SENSE OF PROFOUND

ENNUI

DIPAN KUMAR DAS

SUDIP KUMAR DAS

To those who have felt the weight of emptiness and the pull of profound ennui,

May this exploration offer solace, understanding, and the courage to seek fulfillment.

In memory of the moments lost to listlessness,

And in celebration of the potential for renewal and rediscovery.

This work is dedicated to the resilience of the human spirit

And the enduring pursuit of meaning in a world often shrouded in ennui.

Foreword

In the hustle and bustle of our modern lives, it's easy to overlook the subtle yet profound sensation of ennui that can linger in the background of our existence. Yet, it is this very feeling of emptiness, dissatisfaction, and existential restlessness that often serves as a silent companion, quietly shaping our perceptions, actions, and aspirations.

In "Sense of Profound Ennui," we embark on a journey of introspection and exploration into the depths of ennui - a journey that invites us to confront the complexities of our inner worlds and the challenges of finding meaning and fulfillment in an increasingly interconnected yet disenchanted society.

Through the pages of this book, we delve into the psychology, culture, and evolution of ennui, uncovering its manifestations in the digital age and offering insights into how we might navigate its existential terrain. We confront the paradoxes of our hyperconnected world, where the abundance of information and stimulation can paradoxically lead to a sense of profound disconnection and disillusionment.

Yet, amidst the ennui that pervades our lives, there lies the potential for transformation and renewal. Through self-exploration, pursuit of passion, and embrace of change, we discover pathways to rekindle our sense of purpose and vitality.

As we embark on this exploration, let us heed the call to engage with the ennui that permeates our existence, not as a burden to be avoided, but as a catalyst for growth, understanding, and ultimately, a deeper appreciation of the beauty and complexity of the human experience.

May this book serve as a guidepost for those grappling with the weight of ennui, offering hope, insight, and the reassurance that amidst the depths of existential questioning, there lies the potential for profound transformation and renewal.

Preface

In the course of our lives, we often encounter moments when the world seems to lose its color, when the days blur together in a haze of monotony, and when the pursuit of meaning feels elusive. It is during these moments of profound ennui that we are compelled to pause and reflect on the nature of our existence, to confront the existential questions that linger in the shadows of our consciousness.

"Sense of Profound Ennui" is born out of a deep curiosity about the human condition and a desire to explore the complexities of our inner worlds. As the author of this book, I have been drawn to the enigmatic phenomenon of ennui - a sensation that defies easy categorization yet exerts a powerful influence on our thoughts, emotions, and behaviors.

In the pages that follow, we embark on a multidimensional journey into the heart of ennui, weaving together insights from psychology, philosophy, literature, and cultural analysis. Through this interdisciplinary exploration, we seek to unravel the mysteries of ennui and shed light on its profound significance in our lives.

I invite you, dear reader, to join me on this journey of discovery. Whether you are intimately familiar with the pangs of ennui or are encountering the concept for the first time, my hope is that you will find resonance, illumination, and perhaps even a sense of solace within these pages.

As we navigate the labyrinthine corridors of ennui, let us approach our exploration with open minds and open hearts, embracing the complexities and contradictions that define the human experience. May this book serve as a companion on your own journey of self-discovery and offer guidance as you navigate the ever-shifting landscapes of existence.

Prologue

In the quiet moments before dawn, when the world slumbers and the mind drifts on the edges of consciousness, there exists a space where the weight of existence seems to settle like a heavy mist. It is in these fleeting moments of stillness that the specter of ennui emerges from the shadows, casting its long shadow over the landscape of our thoughts and emotions.

In the prologue of "Sense of Profound Ennui," we find ourselves standing at the threshold of introspection, poised on the brink of a journey into the depths of the human psyche. Here, amidst the silence and the half-light, we confront the enigmatic phenomenon of ennui - that subtle yet pervasive sensation of emptiness, boredom, and existential restlessness that haunts the corridors of our minds.

As we embark on this exploration, we are invited to cast aside preconceptions and assumptions, to relinquish the comfort of certainty in favor of the uncertainty of discovery. For ennui is a riddle wrapped in a mystery, a puzzle whose pieces shift and blur with each passing moment.

In the pages that follow, we will delve into the myriad facets of ennui, tracing its roots in philosophy, psychology, literature, and culture. We will explore its manifestations in the digital age, where the relentless march of progress has given rise to new forms of disconnection and disillusionment.

But amidst the shadows of ennui, there exists a glimmer of hope - a flicker of possibility that beckons us forward. For in the very depths of our existential questioning lies the potential for transformation, for renewal, for the rediscovery of purpose and meaning in a world that often seems indifferent to our struggles.

So let us venture forth, dear reader, into the labyrinthine depths of ennui, guided by curiosity, fueled by wonder, and emboldened by the knowledge that in the pursuit of understanding, we may find solace, clarity, and perhaps even a sense of profound fulfillment.

With that, we turn the page and step into the unknown, ready to confront the mysteries that lie ahead.

Overcoming Ennui And Cultivating Fulfillment

6.

The Evolution Of Ennui

Conclusion:

Embracing the Journey Toward Fulfillment

CHAPTER ONE

Understanding Ennui

Defining Ennui: Exploring the concept of ennui as a profound sense of emptiness, boredom, and dissatisfaction.

Ennui is a complex and multifaceted emotional state characterized by a profound sense of emptiness, boredom, and dissatisfaction. Stemming from the French word for "boredom," ennui encapsulates a deep-seated feeling of weariness and disinterest in life's activities and experiences. It often arises when individuals find themselves disconnected from meaningful engagement or when they perceive a lack of purpose or fulfillment in their daily existence.

At its core, ennui reflects a spiritual or existential malaise, wherein individuals feel detached from their surroundings and disenchanted with the world around them. This sensation of ennui can manifest in various ways, including apathy, lethargy, and a pervasive sense of listlessness. It may also be accompanied by feelings of isolation, alienation, and an inability to derive pleasure or satisfaction from one's pursuits.

Ennui is not merely a fleeting sensation of boredom or restlessness but rather a profound existential condition that can permeate every aspect of an individual's life. It often arises in situations where individuals feel trapped in monotonous routines, devoid of meaningful connections, or lacking in opportunities for personal growth and fulfillment. As a result, ennui can lead to feelings of despair, disillusionment, and a deep-seated longing for something more meaningful or transcendent.

Exploring the concept of ennui requires an examination of its underlying causes and consequences. While external factors such as societal pressures, economic instability, or interpersonal conflicts may contribute to feelings of ennui, it is ultimately an internal state rooted in the individual's perception of their own existence. As such, overcoming ennui often requires a process of introspection, self-discovery, and a reevaluation of one's values, goals, and priorities.

In literature, philosophy, and art, ennui has long been a recurring theme, serving as a lens through which to explore the human condition and the search for meaning in an increasingly complex and fragmented world. From the existentialist writings of Jean-Paul Sartre and Albert Camus to the ennui-laden landscapes depicted by artists like Edward Hopper, ennui continues to captivate and intrigue thinkers and creators alike, offering a poignant reflection on the challenges of modern life and the enduring quest for purpose and fulfillment.

Ennui's continuation through modern times reflects its enduring relevance as a pervasive aspect of the human experience. In today's hyperconnected and fast-paced world, the prevalence of ennui may even be exacerbated by factors such as digital distractions, social media, and a culture of instant gratification. Despite the abundance of stimuli and opportunities for entertainment, many individuals still find themselves grappling with feelings of emptiness and disillusionment.

Moreover, the COVID-19 pandemic and its associated disruptions have further underscored the existential dimensions of ennui. Lockdowns, social distancing measures, and economic uncertainty have intensified feelings of isolation and alienation for many people, exacerbating existential angst and prompting a collective reevaluation of life's priorities and meaning.

In response to the challenges posed by ennui, individuals may adopt various coping mechanisms, ranging from seeking out novel experiences and pursuing new interests to engaging in introspective practices such as meditation or therapy. Additionally, cultivating meaningful connections with others, fostering a sense of community, and finding purpose in work or creative endeavors can help alleviate feelings of ennui and foster a deeper sense of fulfillment and satisfaction.

From a societal standpoint, addressing the underlying causes of ennui requires a holistic approach that acknowledges the interplay between individual well-being, social structures, and cultural values. This may involve initiatives aimed at promoting work-life balance, fostering inclusive communities, and reimagining systems of education and employment to better align with individuals' aspirations and values.

Ultimately, exploring the concept of ennui invites us to confront the existential challenges of modern life and to reflect on the ways in which we can cultivate meaning, connection, and fulfillment in the face of adversity. By embracing introspection, creativity, and a spirit of inquiry, we can navigate the depths of ennui and emerge with a renewed sense of purpose and vitality.

Furthermore, the exploration of ennui prompts a reconsideration of societal values and structures that may contribute to its prevalence. In contemporary consumerist cultures, for instance, there is often an emphasis on material wealth, status, and external markers of success. This emphasis can lead individuals to pursue goals and lifestyles that are ultimately unfulfilling, contributing to feelings of ennui when the promised rewards fail to satisfy deeper existential needs.

Similarly, the digital age has ushered in an era of constant connectivity and information overload, which can paradoxically exacerbate feelings of disconnection and alienation. The relentless barrage of notifications, the pressure to curate online personas, and the comparison with others' seemingly perfect lives on social media platforms can foster a sense of inadequacy and ennui, as individuals struggle to find authenticity and meaning amid the virtual noise.

In light of these challenges, there is a growing recognition of the importance of fostering a more holistic and sustainable approach to well-being—one that prioritizes inner fulfillment, meaningful relationships, and a sense of belonging. This may involve cultivating practices of mindfulness, gratitude, and self-reflection, as well as fostering genuine connections with others and nurturing a sense of community and belonging.

From a broader societal perspective, addressing ennui necessitates a reevaluation of cultural narratives and social structures that perpetuate a narrow definition of success and happiness. By promoting values such as empathy, compassion, and altruism, and by designing environments that prioritize human flourishing over relentless productivity, societies can create conditions that support individuals in leading more meaningful and fulfilling lives.

In essence, the exploration of ennui invites us to confront the existential dimensions of human existence and to reflect on the ways in which we can cultivate deeper connections, purpose, and fulfillment in our lives. By embracing vulnerability, authenticity, and a willingness to engage with life's inherent uncertainties, we can transcend the emptiness of ennui and discover a profound sense of meaning and vitality.

Historical Perspectives: Tracing the roots of ennui in philosophy, literature, and psychology.

Tracing the roots of ennui in philosophy, literature, and psychology reveals its longstanding presence as a theme deeply intertwined with the human experience:

Philosophy:

Existentialism: Philosophers such as Jean-Paul Sartre and Albert Camus explored ennui as a fundamental aspect of existential angst. In Sartre's existentialist philosophy, ennui arises from the confrontation with one's own freedom and the responsibility to create meaning in a seemingly absurd world. Camus, in "The Myth of Sisyphus," portrays the eternal struggle against ennui as part of the human condition.

Nihilism: Friedrich Nietzsche examined the nihilistic aspects of ennui, viewing it as a symptom of the "death of God" and the erosion of traditional values. For Nietzsche, overcoming ennui requires a radical revaluation of values and the creation of one's own meaning in a world devoid of inherent significance.

Stoicism: Stoic philosophers like Seneca and Epictetus offered strategies for coping with ennui through practices such as mindfulness, acceptance of fate, and focusing on what is within one's control. Stoicism emphasizes cultivating inner resilience and finding contentment in the present moment, even in the face of adversity.

Literature:

Romanticism: Writers of the Romantic era, such as Lord Byron and Percy Bysshe Shelley, often depicted ennui as a consequence of disillusionment with society's constraints and the inability to reconcile inner desires with external reality. Romantic literature frequently explores themes of longing, melancholy, and the quest for transcendent experiences.

Realism and Modernism: Authors like Gustave Flaubert ("Madame Bovary"), Leo Tolstoy ("Anna Karenina"), and Fyodor Dostoevsky ("Notes from Underground") portrayed ennui as a prevalent condition in the modern world, reflecting the disintegration of traditional values and the alienating effects of urbanization and industrialization.

Absurdist Literature: Writers such as Franz Kafka ("The Metamorphosis") and Samuel Beckett ("Waiting for Godot") delved into the absurdity of existence and the futility of human endeavors, capturing the sense of existential ennui that permeates modern life.

Psychology:

Psychoanalysis: Sigmund Freud and later psychologists explored ennui as a psychological phenomenon linked to repressed desires, unresolved conflicts, and the search for pleasure. Freudian theory suggests that ennui may arise when individuals are unable to satisfy their unconscious drives or when they experience a disconnect between their conscious goals and deeper instincts.

Positive Psychology: Contemporary psychologists like Mihaly Csikszentmihalyi and Martin Seligman have investigated the concept of "flow," a state of optimal engagement and fulfillment characterized by deep concentration and a sense of purpose. Understanding flow offers insights into combating ennui by fostering experiences that promote intrinsic motivation and personal growth.

Through these philosophical, literary, and psychological perspectives, ennui emerges as a rich and multifaceted phenomenon that reflects humanity's ongoing struggle to find meaning, purpose, and fulfillment in an ever-changing world.

Modern Manifestations: Analyzing how ennui manifests in contemporary society amidst technological advancements and societal changes.

In contemporary society, ennui manifests in nuanced ways shaped by technological advancements, societal changes, and cultural shifts. Here's an analysis of some modern manifestations of ennui:

Digital Distraction and Overstimulation:

Social Media Fatigue: While social media platforms offer connectivity and entertainment, they can also contribute to feelings of ennui. Endless scrolling, constant notifications, and curated portrayals of others' lives can lead to a sense of disconnection and dissatisfaction.

Information Overload: The abundance of information available online can overwhelm individuals, leading to a sense of mental fatigue and apathy. Paradoxically, despite access to vast knowledge, many may feel directionless and unfulfilled.

Alienation and Disconnect:

Virtual Relationships: Despite digital connectivity, individuals may still experience a profound sense of loneliness and alienation, especially if online interactions lack depth and authenticity. The superficiality of virtual connections can exacerbate feelings of emptiness and disconnection.

Urban Isolation: In densely populated urban environments, individuals may feel anonymous and disconnected from their surroundings, leading to a sense of ennui rooted in a lack of meaningful social connections and a feeling of insignificance in the crowd.

Consumerism and Materialism:

Hedonic Treadmill: The pursuit of material possessions and external markers of success can result in a cycle of fleeting gratification followed by a return to a baseline state of dissatisfaction. This "hedonic treadmill" perpetuates ennui as individuals constantly seek new sources of stimulation and validation.

Choice Paralysis: The abundance of consumer choices can lead to decision fatigue and a sense of existential ennui. Paralyzed by the fear of making the wrong choice or the inability to discern meaningful options, individuals may feel overwhelmed and indecisive.

Work and Career:

Job Dissatisfaction: Despite technological advancements and increased productivity, many individuals experience ennui in their professional lives. Monotonous tasks, lack of autonomy, and a sense of purposelessness can contribute to feelings of boredom and disengagement at work.

Gig Economy Uncertainty: In the gig economy, where precarious employment is common, individuals may grapple with feelings of instability and existential angst. The absence of long-term career prospects and financial security can exacerbate ennui as individuals navigate uncertain futures.

Environmental Concerns:

Climate Anxiety: The looming threat of climate change and environmental degradation can evoke feelings of helplessness and despair, contributing to a sense of existential ennui. The enormity of the challenge and the slow pace of collective action may lead to a sense of futility and resignation.

Erosion of Traditional Structures:

Decline of Community: Traditional forms of community and social cohesion are increasingly fragmented, leading to a sense of rootlessness and ennui. The erosion of neighborhood bonds and extended family networks can leave individuals feeling isolated and disconnected from meaningful sources of support.

Loss of Meaningful Rituals: Modern society often lacks the rich tapestry of rituals and rites of passage that once provided structure and meaning to life. The absence of ceremonies marking significant life events can contribute to a sense of ennui and existential aimlessness.

Understanding these modern manifestations of ennui is crucial for addressing its underlying causes and cultivating environments that foster meaning, connection, and fulfillment in contemporary society. By recognizing the impact of technological, societal, and cultural factors on individual well-being, we can work towards mitigating the pervasive sense of emptiness and disconnection that characterizes ennui in the modern age.

CHAPTER TWO

The Psychology of Ennui

Psychological Factors: Examining the psychological underpinnings of ennui, including existential angst, lack of purpose, and disconnection.

The psychological underpinnings of ennui encompass a complex interplay of existential angst, lack of purpose, and disconnection from oneself, others, and the world at large:

Existential Angst:

Freedom and Responsibility: Existential philosophers such as Jean-Paul Sartre and Albert Camus emphasized the inherent freedom and responsibility of individuals to create meaning in a seemingly indifferent universe. However, this freedom can also lead to anxiety and uncertainty, as individuals grapple with the burden of defining their own values and purpose.

Absurdity of Existence: Existentialists contend that life is inherently absurd, devoid of inherent meaning or purpose. Confronted with the absurdity of existence, individuals may experience feelings of ennui as they struggle to find significance in a world that appears indifferent to their desires and aspirations.

Lack of Purpose:

Meaninglessness: Ennui often arises from a perceived lack of purpose or direction in life. When individuals feel disconnected from meaningful goals and pursuits, they may experience a sense of emptiness and aimlessness, characterized by a pervasive feeling of dissatisfaction with the status quo.

Alienation from Work: In contemporary society, many individuals experience ennui in their professional lives, where monotonous tasks and a lack of autonomy contribute to a sense of disengagement and disillusionment. Without a sense of purpose or fulfillment in their work, individuals may struggle to find meaning in their daily activities.

Disconnection:

Social Isolation: Feelings of ennui can be exacerbated by social isolation and a lack of meaningful connections with others. In an age of digital communication and superficial interactions, individuals may yearn for genuine intimacy and authentic relationships, leading to a sense of alienation and disconnect.

Alienation from Self: Ennui may also stem from a disconnect from one's own thoughts, emotions, and desires. When individuals feel disconnected from their inner selves and lack a sense of self-awareness and authenticity, they may experience a profound sense of emptiness and disorientation.

Cognitive Factors:

Rumination: Individuals prone to rumination—repetitive and negative thinking patterns—may be more susceptible to feelings of ennui. Rumination can exacerbate existential concerns and lead to a cycle of introspective brooding, amplifying feelings of emptiness and dissatisfaction.

Comparison: Social comparison, particularly facilitated by social media, can contribute to feelings of ennui by fostering a sense of inadequacy and unmet desires. Constantly comparing oneself to others' curated lives can perpetuate a sense of discontent and disconnection from one's own experiences.

Understanding these psychological factors is essential for addressing and mitigating feelings of ennui. By fostering self-awareness, cultivating meaningful connections, and exploring avenues for personal growth and fulfillment, individuals can navigate the existential challenges of modern life and find deeper meaning and satisfaction in their existence.

Neurological Insights: Investigating the brain mechanisms associated with ennui and its impact on cognitive processes.

Investigating the neurological mechanisms associated with ennui offers insights into its impact on cognitive processes and subjective experiences. While research on this specific topic is limited, several brain regions and neural processes are likely involved:

Default Mode Network (DMN):

The DMN is a network of brain regions that becomes active when individuals are not focused on the external environment or engaged in specific tasks. It is implicated in self-referential processing, mind-wandering, and introspection.

Ennui may involve heightened activity in the DMN, as individuals ruminate on existential concerns, dwell on feelings of boredom or dissatisfaction, or engage in repetitive and negative thought patterns.

Prefrontal Cortex (PFC):

The PFC plays a crucial role in executive functions such as decision-making, goal-setting, and planning. It is involved in evaluating the significance of stimuli, regulating emotions, and maintaining attention.

Ennui may be associated with reduced activity or dysregulation in the PFC, leading to difficulties in setting and pursuing meaningful goals, making decisions, and maintaining focus and motivation.

Reward Circuitry:

The brain's reward circuitry, including regions such as the nucleus accumbens and ventral tegmental area, is involved in processing pleasurable stimuli and motivating behavior.

Ennui may arise from dysregulation or desensitization of the reward system, leading to a reduced capacity to experience pleasure or derive satisfaction from activities that were once rewarding.

Dopamine System:

Dopamine is a neurotransmitter associated with motivation, reward, and reinforcement learning. Dysregulation of the dopamine system has been implicated in various mood disorders and motivational deficits.

Ennui may involve alterations in dopamine signaling, resulting in diminished motivation, reduced responsiveness to positive stimuli, and anhedonia (the inability to experience pleasure).

Serotonin System:

Serotonin is another neurotransmitter involved in mood regulation, cognition, and behavior. Dysregulation of the serotonin system has been linked to depressive symptoms and feelings of malaise.

Ennui may be associated with disruptions in serotonin signaling, contributing to feelings of lethargy, low mood, and a general sense of dissatisfaction with life.

Neuroplasticity:

Chronic experiences of ennui may impact brain structure and function through neuroplastic changes, altering neural circuits involved in emotion regulation, motivation, and cognitive processing.

Conversely, interventions aimed at alleviating ennui, such as cognitive-behavioral therapy, mindfulness practices, or engaging in novel experiences, may promote neuroplasticity and support adaptive changes in brain function.

Further research is needed to elucidate the specific neural mechanisms underlying ennui and its effects on cognitive processes. By understanding the neurological basis of ennui, researchers may develop targeted interventions to alleviate its symptoms and promote well-being and fulfillment.

Coping Mechanisms: Exploring various coping strategies individuals employ to alleviate feelings of ennui, such as mindfulness, creativity, and seeking novelty.

Individuals employ a variety of coping strategies to alleviate feelings of ennui and find meaning, purpose, and fulfillment in their lives. Here are some common coping mechanisms:

Mindfulness and Meditation:

Practicing mindfulness involves paying attention to the present moment without judgment. Mindfulness meditation techniques, such as focused breathing or body scanning, can help individuals cultivate awareness, reduce rumination, and find acceptance in the here and now.

By grounding themselves in the present moment, individuals can break free from the cycle of repetitive and negative thought patterns that contribute to feelings of ennui.

Engagement in Creative Activities:

Creativity offers a means of self-expression, exploration, and discovery. Engaging in creative pursuits such as writing, painting, music, or crafting can provide a sense of purpose, flow, and satisfaction.

Creative activities allow individuals to tap into their inner resources, connect with their passions, and transcend feelings of emptiness by channeling their energy into meaningful endeavors.

Seeking Novelty and Exploration:

Introducing novelty into one's life can stimulate curiosity, excitement, and a sense of adventure. Exploring new interests, hobbies, or environments can break the monotony of routine and inject vitality into daily experiences.

By stepping outside of their comfort zones and embracing new challenges, individuals can reignite their zest for life and rediscover a sense of wonder and possibility.

Cultivating Meaningful Connections:

Building and nurturing meaningful relationships with others is essential for combating feelings of isolation and disconnection. Spending quality time with loved ones, engaging in deep conversations, and offering support can foster a sense of belonging and connectedness.

Meaningful connections provide emotional support, validation, and a sense of shared purpose, helping individuals navigate the challenges of ennui with resilience and mutual understanding.

Physical Activity and Exercise:

Physical activity has numerous benefits for mental health and well-being. Regular exercise releases endorphins, reduces stress, and enhances mood, providing a natural antidote to feelings of ennui.

Whether through vigorous workouts, outdoor activities, or simply going for a walk, engaging in physical exercise can boost energy levels, increase vitality, and promote a sense of aliveness and vitality.

Self-Exploration and Personal Growth:

Engaging in self-reflection, introspection, and personal growth practices can help individuals clarify their values, goals, and priorities. Journaling, therapy, or participating in self-help workshops can facilitate greater self-awareness and empowerment.

By embarking on a journey of self-discovery and personal development, individuals can find meaning and purpose in their lives, transcending ennui and embracing a deeper sense of fulfillment.

By employing these coping mechanisms, individuals can navigate the challenges of ennui and cultivate resilience, vitality, and well-being. Each person may find different strategies that resonate with them personally, emphasizing the importance of self-awareness and experimentation in finding effective ways to alleviate feelings of emptiness and dissatisfaction.

CHAPTER THREE

Cultural Perspectives on Ennui

Literary Explorations: Delving into how ennui is depicted in literature, art, and cinema across different cultures and time periods.

Ennui has been a recurring theme in literature, art, and cinema across different cultures and time periods, reflecting the universal human experience of existential angst, boredom, and dissatisfaction. Here's a brief exploration of how ennui is depicted in each of these mediums:

Literature:

19th Century Literature: Writers such as Gustave Flaubert ("Madame Bovary"), Leo Tolstoy ("Anna Karenina"), and Charles Baudelaire ("The Flowers of Evil") depicted ennui as a prevalent condition in bourgeois society, characterized by disillusionment, longing, and a sense of existential emptiness.

Modernist Literature: Authors like Franz Kafka ("The Metamorphosis"), Virginia Woolf ("Mrs. Dalloway"), and Albert Camus ("The Stranger") explored themes of alienation, absurdity, and ennui in the context of modernity and the breakdown of traditional values.

Postmodern Literature: Postmodern writers, such as Don DeLillo ("White Noise") and Haruki Murakami ("Norwegian Wood"), continued to probe the existential dimensions of ennui, often through fragmented narratives and surreal imagery.

Art:

Realism and Impressionism: Artists like Edouard Manet, Edgar Degas, and Gustave Caillebotte depicted scenes of urban ennui and leisure in 19th-century Paris, capturing the ennui-laden atmosphere of modern life.

Expressionism: Expressionist painters, such as Edvard Munch and Egon Schiele, delved into the inner turmoil and psychological angst of the human condition, conveying feelings of existential alienation and despair.

Surrealism: Surrealist artists, including Salvador Dalí and René Magritte, explored the subconscious mind and the irrational forces underlying human existence, often portraying dreamlike landscapes imbued with a sense of ennui and dislocation.

Cinema:

French New Wave: Filmmakers like Jean-Luc Godard ("Breathless") and François Truffaut

("The 400 Blows") captured the ennui of postwar youth in France, depicting aimless characters adrift in a world of existential uncertainty and disillusionment.

Japanese Cinema: Directors such as Yasujirō Ozu ("Tokyo Story") and Akira Kurosawa ("Ikiru") examined themes of ennui, alienation, and mortality in postwar Japan, exploring the tension between tradition and modernity.

American Cinema: Filmmakers like Billy Wilder ("The Apartment"), Stanley Kubrick ("2001: A Space Odyssey"), and Sofia Coppola ("Lost in Translation") portrayed ennui as a pervasive condition in contemporary American society, characterized by ennui-laden landscapes and characters searching for meaning in an indifferent world.

Across literature, art, and cinema, ennui serves as a rich and multifaceted theme that reflects humanity's ongoing quest for meaning, connection, and fulfillment amidst the complexities of modern life. Whether portrayed in the stark realism of a 19th-century novel, the vibrant colors of an impressionist painting, or the existential despair of a postmodern film, ennui continues to captivate and intrigue audiences, offering a poignant reflection on the human condition.

Russian Literature:

Russian literature, particularly in the 19th and early 20th centuries, often delves deeply into themes of ennui and existential angst. Fyodor Dostoevsky's "Notes from Underground" explores the psychological turmoil and alienation of a disillusioned narrator, while Anton Chekhov's short stories, such as "The Lady with the Dog," depict characters grappling with feelings of emptiness and dissatisfaction in their lives.

German Literature:

German literature, especially during the Romantic and Expressionist periods, frequently explores the darker aspects of the human psyche. In Franz Kafka's works, such as "The Trial" and "The Castle," characters navigate bureaucratic absurdity and existential uncertainty, reflecting feelings of ennui and alienation in the face of an incomprehensible world.

Japanese Literature:

Japanese literature often examines ennui in the context of societal expectations and cultural norms. Haruki Murakami's novels, such as "Norwegian Wood" and "Kafka on the Shore," feature characters grappling with feelings of disconnection and longing in contemporary Japan, while Yukio Mishima's works, such as "The Sailor Who Fell from Grace with the Sea," delve into themes of existential despair and nihilism.

Visual Arts:

In addition to the movements mentioned earlier, various art movements have explored ennui in different ways. The Pop Art of the 1960s, with artists like Andy Warhol and Roy

Lichtenstein, often critiqued consumer culture and the banality of everyday life. Contemporary artists, such as Damien Hirst and Tracey Emin, continue to explore themes of ennui, isolation, and existential dread in their works.

Cinema in Other Cultures:

Ennui is also a prominent theme in cinema from other parts of the world. For example, Italian Neorealism, with films like Vittorio De Sica's "Bicycle Thieves," portrays the ennui of post-war Italy through the lens of everyday struggles and disillusionment. Iranian cinema, including works by directors like Abbas Kiarostami and Asghar Farhadi, often explores ennui in the context of social and political repression.

In sum, across diverse cultures and time periods, ennui remains a prevalent and resonant theme in literature, art, and cinema. Whether portrayed through the existential despair of a Russian novel, the existential absurdity of a Kafkaesque narrative, or the alienation of a contemporary film, ennui serves as a mirror to humanity's collective search for meaning, connection, and transcendence in an uncertain world.

some famous dialogues from cinema that touch upon themes of ennui and existential angst:

"The 400 Blows" (1959), directed by François Truffaut:

Dialogue: "I'm bored, bored, bored!"

"Breathless" (1960), directed by Jean-Luc Godard:

Dialogue: "What's your greatest ambition in life?" "To become immortal... and then die."

"Lost in Translation" (2003), directed by Sofia Coppola:

Dialogue: "The most terrifying day of your life is the day the first one is born." "Nobody ever tells you that."

"Annie Hall" (1977), directed by Woody Allen:

Dialogue: "There's an old joke. Uh, two elderly women are at a Catskills mountain resort, and one of 'em says, 'Boy, the food at this place is really terrible.' The other one says, 'Yeah, I know; and such small portions.'"

"Fight Club" (1999), directed by David Fincher:

Dialogue: "This is your life, and it's ending one minute at a time."

"Taxi Driver" (1976), directed by Martin Scorsese:

Dialogue: "Loneliness has followed me my whole life, everywhere. In bars, in cars, sidewalks, stores, everywhere. There's no escape. I'm God's lonely man."

"Eternal Sunshine of the Spotless Mind" (2004), directed by Michel Gondry:

Dialogue: "Too many guys think I'm a concept, or I complete them, or I'm gonna make them alive. But I'm just a fucked-up girl who's lookin' for my own peace of mind; don't assign me yours."

These dialogues capture the sense of ennui, disillusionment, and existential questioning that pervades many films exploring the human condition. They reflect characters' struggles with boredom, loneliness, and the search for meaning in a seemingly indifferent world.

Societal Influences: Analyzing how cultural norms, socioeconomic factors, and technological advancements contribute to the prevalence of ennui in society.

The prevalence of ennui in society can be influenced by a multitude of factors, including cultural norms, socioeconomic conditions, and technological advancements. Here's an analysis of how each of these factors contributes to the experience of ennui:

Cultural Norms:

Consumerist Culture: In societies that prioritize material wealth, status, and external markers of success, individuals may feel pressured to constantly pursue new experiences and possessions in search of fulfillment. However, this emphasis on consumption can lead to a sense of emptiness and dissatisfaction when material goods fail to provide lasting happiness.

Workaholic Mentality: Cultures that glorify productivity and busyness may contribute to feelings of ennui by fostering a relentless pursuit of achievement and external validation. Individuals may become trapped in monotonous routines and long hours of work, sacrificing personal well-being and leisure time in the process.

Socioeconomic Factors:

Income Inequality: Socioeconomic disparities can exacerbate feelings of ennui, particularly among marginalized communities who may lack access to resources and opportunities for personal fulfillment. Economic instability and financial insecurity can contribute to a sense of hopelessness and disillusionment with societal structures.

Job Insecurity: In an era of globalization and automation, many individuals face precarious employment conditions, characterized by temporary contracts, gig work, and lack of job security. The uncertainty surrounding employment prospects can lead to feelings of ennui and existential angst about the future.

Technological Advancements:

Digital Distraction: While technology offers unprecedented access to information and connectivity, it also fosters a culture of constant distraction and superficial engagement. Social media, in particular, can contribute to feelings of ennui by promoting comparison, validation-seeking behaviors, and passive consumption of content.

24/7 Connectivity: The blurring of boundaries between work and leisure in the digital age can lead to feelings of ennui as individuals struggle to disconnect and find moments of genuine rest and relaxation. The pressure to be constantly available and productive can detract from opportunities for meaningful engagement and fulfillment.

Urbanization and Modernization:

Urban Isolation: Rapid urbanization and the breakdown of traditional community structures can contribute to feelings of alienation and disconnection from others. In densely populated cities, individuals may feel anonymous and disconnected, leading to a sense of ennui and existential isolation.

Loss of Rituals and Traditions: The erosion of rituals and traditions that once provided meaning and coherence to life can exacerbate feelings of ennui in modern society. Without shared cultural practices to anchor individuals to their communities and identities, they may experience a sense of rootlessness and existential disorientation.

In summary, cultural norms, socioeconomic conditions, technological advancements, and urbanization all play significant roles in shaping the prevalence of ennui in society. By recognizing the societal influences that contribute to feelings of emptiness and dissatisfaction, individuals and communities can work towards cultivating environments that promote genuine connection, purpose, and well-being.

Cross-Cultural Variances: Examining how perceptions and experiences of ennui vary across different cultural contexts and societies.

Perceptions and experiences of ennui can indeed vary significantly across different cultural contexts and societies due to diverse social, economic, and philosophical factors. Here's an examination of some key cross-cultural variances:

Cultural Attitudes Toward Leisure:

In some cultures, such as those with a strong work ethic like the United States or South Korea, leisure time may be viewed as unproductive or even wasteful, leading to feelings of guilt or ennui during downtime. In contrast, cultures with a more balanced approach to work and leisure, such as those in Southern Europe or Latin America, may prioritize relaxation and socializing, reducing the likelihood of experiencing ennui during periods of rest.

Collectivism vs. Individualism:

Cultures that emphasize collectivism, such as many East Asian societies, may prioritize social harmony and conformity over individual autonomy. In such cultures, individuals may experience ennui as a result of feeling constrained by societal expectations and norms. Conversely, cultures that emphasize individualism, such as those in Western Europe and North America, may experience ennui as a consequence of the existential freedom and responsibility that accompany individual autonomy.

Spiritual and Philosophical Traditions:

Societies with strong spiritual or philosophical traditions, such as those in India or Japan, may offer alternative frameworks for understanding and coping with ennui. Practices such as meditation, mindfulness, or acceptance of impermanence (e.g., Buddhist teachings on the nature of suffering) can provide individuals with tools for transcending feelings of emptiness and finding peace amidst existential uncertainty.

Historical and Socioeconomic Context:

The historical and socioeconomic context of a society can influence the prevalence and experience of ennui. For example, in post-industrial societies where basic needs are more easily met, individuals may have greater opportunities for leisure and self-exploration, but may also be more prone to feelings of existential dissatisfaction due to the lack of clear societal roles and structures.

Cultural Expressions:

The portrayal of ennui in art, literature, and media can vary across cultures, reflecting different cultural values, norms, and aesthetic sensibilities. For example, Japanese literature often depicts ennui in subtle and understated ways, reflecting the cultural value of restraint and introspection, while Western literature may approach the theme with more overt existential angst and introspection.

Social Support and Community Cohesion:

Cultures with strong social support networks and tight-knit communities may provide individuals with a sense of belonging and connection, reducing the likelihood of experiencing ennui. In contrast, cultures characterized by social fragmentation and individualism may leave individuals feeling isolated and disconnected, increasing susceptibility to feelings of existential emptiness.

Overall, perceptions and experiences of ennui are shaped by a complex interplay of cultural, social, economic, and philosophical factors.

By acknowledging and understanding these cross-cultural variances, we can gain insight into the diverse ways in which individuals around the world navigate the existential challenges of modern life.

CHAPTER FOUR

Navigating Ennui in the Digital Age

Technology and Ennui: Investigating the impact of digital culture, social media, and constant connectivity on feelings of ennui and existential restlessness.

The impact of digital culture, social media, and constant connectivity on feelings of ennui and existential restlessness is profound and multifaceted. Here's an investigation into how these technological advancements contribute to the experience of ennui:

Constant Stimulation and Distraction:

Digital culture bombards individuals with a constant stream of information, entertainment, and social interactions. While this may initially provide a sense of stimulation and engagement, it can also lead to feelings of ennui as individuals become accustomed to instant gratification and novelty, making it difficult to find lasting satisfaction in any one experience.

Comparison and Validation-Seeking Behaviors:

Social media platforms facilitate the constant comparison of one's life and achievements with others, leading to feelings of inadequacy and existential restlessness. The curated nature of social media feeds often presents an unrealistic portrayal of others' lives, fueling a sense of FOMO (fear of missing out) and perpetuating a cycle of validation-seeking behaviors.

Shallow Relationships and Disconnection:

Despite the illusion of connectivity, digital communication often lacks depth and authenticity, leading to a sense of disconnection and loneliness. Superficial interactions on social media may exacerbate feelings of ennui by failing to fulfill the need for genuine human connection and intimacy.

Attention Fragmentation and Information Overload:

The constant barrage of notifications, emails, and messages can overwhelm individuals, leading to a sense of cognitive overload and mental fatigue. This continuous partial attention to multiple stimuli can detract from the ability to engage in deep, meaningful experiences, contributing to feelings of ennui and existential restlessness.

Loss of Presence and Mindfulness:

Digital culture encourages constant multitasking and divided attention, making it difficult for individuals to be fully present in the moment and engage in mindful activities.

Without opportunities for introspection and contemplation, individuals may struggle to find meaning and fulfillment in their lives, leading to feelings of ennui and disconnection from the self.

Escapism and Avoidance:

Digital technology offers endless opportunities for escapism through entertainment, gaming, and online consumption. While these activities may provide temporary relief from feelings of ennui, they can also perpetuate a cycle of avoidance and disengagement from reality, ultimately exacerbating existential restlessness and dissatisfaction.

In summary, digital culture, social media, and constant connectivity can exacerbate feelings of ennui and existential restlessness by promoting constant stimulation, comparison, and distraction, while undermining genuine human connection, presence, and mindfulness. Recognizing the impact of these technological advancements is crucial for fostering environments that support authentic connection, meaningful engagement, and inner fulfillment in the digital age.

Digital Detox: Discussing the importance of disconnecting from technology and engaging in offline activities to combat ennui and restore a sense of fulfillment.

Engaging in a digital detox—disconnecting from technology and embracing offline activities—can play a vital role in combating ennui and restoring a sense of fulfillment in today's hyperconnected world. Here's why it's important:

Promotes Mindfulness and Presence:

Disconnecting from technology allows individuals to be fully present in the moment and engage more deeply with their surroundings. By cultivating mindfulness and awareness, individuals can appreciate the beauty of the present moment and find meaning in everyday experiences, mitigating feelings of ennui and existential restlessness.

Fosters Authentic Connections:

Offline activities such as face-to-face conversations, shared meals, and outdoor adventures provide opportunities for genuine human connection and intimacy. Building meaningful relationships and engaging in real-life interactions can alleviate feelings of loneliness and disconnection, fostering a sense of belonging and fulfillment.

Encourages Creative Expression:

Unplugging from technology frees up time and mental space for creative pursuits such as writing, drawing, or playing music. Engaging in creative activities allows individuals to express themselves authentically, tap into their inner resources, and cultivate a sense of purpose and accomplishment, counteracting feelings of ennui and existential restlessness.

Supports Physical Health and Well-being:

Excessive screen time and sedentary behavior associated with digital technology can have detrimental effects on physical health and well-being. Disconnecting from technology encourages individuals to engage in physical activities such as exercise, outdoor recreation, or hobbies, promoting overall health and vitality.

Facilitates Self-Reflection and Personal Growth:

Without the constant distraction of digital devices, individuals have the opportunity to engage in self-reflection, introspection, and contemplation. Disconnecting from technology allows for moments of solitude and silence, enabling individuals to connect with their inner selves, clarify their values and goals, and cultivate a deeper sense of self-awareness and fulfillment.

Restores Balance and Perspective:

In a digital world characterized by information overload and constant connectivity, a digital detox offers a respite from the demands of technology and restores balance to individuals' lives. By stepping back from the digital realm, individuals can gain perspective on their priorities, reassess their relationship with technology, and reclaim agency over how they spend their time and energy.

In conclusion, embracing a digital detox is essential for combating ennui and restoring a sense of fulfillment in the modern age. By disconnecting from technology and embracing offline activities, individuals can cultivate mindfulness, foster authentic connections, unleash creativity, support physical health, facilitate personal growth, and restore balance to their lives, ultimately finding greater meaning and fulfillment in the process.

Reconnecting with Meaning: Exploring how individuals can rediscover purpose and meaning in a hyperconnected world by fostering authentic connections, pursuing passions, and engaging in meaningful activities.

In a hyperconnected world where distractions abound, rediscovering purpose and meaning requires intentional efforts to foster authentic connections, pursue passions, and engage in meaningful activities. Here's how individuals can reconnect with meaning:

Cultivate Authentic Connections:

Prioritize quality over quantity in relationships, nurturing genuine connections with family, friends, and community members. Invest time and energy in building deep, meaningful relationships based on trust, empathy, and mutual support.

Engage in meaningful conversations that foster understanding, connection, and vulnerability. Listen actively, share openly, and cultivate empathy and compassion for others' experiences and perspectives.

Seek out opportunities for collaboration and shared experiences, whether through volunteering, joining community groups, or participating in group activities that align with personal values and interests.

Pursue Passions and Interests:

Identify passions, hobbies, and interests that bring joy, fulfillment, and a sense of purpose. Explore new activities, skills, and experiences that resonate with personal values and aspirations.

Dedicate time and resources to pursuing passions, whether it's through creative expression, outdoor adventures, or intellectual pursuits. Embrace curiosity and experimentation, and don't be afraid to take risks or step outside of your comfort zone.

Cultivate a growth mindset, viewing challenges and setbacks as opportunities for learning and growth. Celebrate progress and small victories along the way, and savor the journey of self-discovery and exploration.

Engage in Meaningful Activities:

Seek out activities and experiences that align with personal values and contribute to a sense of fulfillment and purpose. Whether it's volunteering for a cause you believe in, participating in cultural events, or immersing yourself in nature, prioritize activities that bring a sense of meaning and connection.

Practice mindfulness and presence in everyday activities, savoring moments of beauty, gratitude, and wonder. Engage fully in the present moment, whether it's enjoying a meal with loved ones, appreciating nature's beauty, or pursuing creative endeavors.

Reflect on personal values, goals, and aspirations, and align daily actions with overarching principles and priorities. Cultivate a sense of intentionality and purpose in how you spend your time and energy, making conscious choices that contribute to a meaningful and fulfilling life.

Find Meaning in Service and Contribution:

Explore opportunities for service and contribution to others, whether through acts of kindness, volunteering, or advocating for social change. Engage in activities that promote the well-being of others and contribute to a sense of connection and shared humanity.

Reflect on the impact of your actions and choices on others and the broader community. Recognize the ripple effect of small acts of kindness and compassion, and find meaning in the interconnectedness of all beings.

Cultivate a sense of purpose beyond individual fulfillment, recognizing the importance of contributing to something larger than oneself and leaving a positive legacy for future generations.

In summary, reconnecting with meaning in a hyperconnected world requires a conscious commitment to fostering authentic connections, pursuing passions, engaging in meaningful activities, and finding purpose in service and contribution to others. By prioritizing authenticity, curiosity, and intentionality in daily life, individuals can rediscover a sense of purpose and fulfillment amidst the distractions and demands of modern society.

CHAPTER FIVE

Overcoming Ennui and Cultivating Fulfillment

Self-Exploration: Encouraging readers to engage in introspection and self-reflection to identify underlying causes of ennui and areas for personal growth.

Encouraging readers to engage in introspection and self-reflection is crucial for identifying underlying causes of ennui and areas for personal growth. Here's how individuals can embark on a journey of self-exploration:

Create Space for Reflection:

Set aside dedicated time and space for introspection and self-reflection. Find a quiet and comfortable environment where you can disconnect from distractions and focus inwardly.

Consider incorporating mindfulness practices such as meditation, journaling, or deep breathing exercises to cultivate awareness and presence in the moment.

Ask Meaningful Questions:

Reflect on your values, beliefs, and aspirations. What truly matters to you in life? What brings you a sense of joy, purpose, and fulfillment?

Explore the underlying emotions and experiences that may be contributing to feelings of ennui. Are there unresolved issues, unmet needs, or areas of dissatisfaction in your life?

Consider your past experiences, relationships, and life choices. What lessons have you learned from your successes and failures? How have these experiences shaped your identity and worldview?

Explore Core Beliefs and Assumptions:

Examine the beliefs and assumptions that may be influencing your thoughts, emotions, and behaviors. Are there limiting beliefs or negative self-talk patterns that are holding you back from living authentically and pursuing your goals?

Challenge assumptions about success, happiness, and fulfillment that may be rooted in societal expectations or cultural norms. What does success mean to you, and how do you define a meaningful life on your own terms?

Identify Areas for Growth and Development:

Acknowledge areas of your life where you feel stagnant, unfulfilled, or disconnected. What aspects of your life are in need of attention and nurturing?

Consider your strengths, talents, and passions. How can you leverage these assets to pursue meaningful goals and contribute to the world in a positive way?

Embrace a growth mindset, viewing challenges and setbacks as opportunities for learning and self-improvement. What steps can you take to overcome obstacles and cultivate resilience in the face of adversity?

Set Intentions and Take Action:

Based on your reflections, set intentions for personal growth and development. What specific changes or actions can you commit to in order to align your life more closely with your values and aspirations?

Break down larger goals into manageable steps and create a plan of action to achieve them. Hold yourself accountable and track your progress over time.

Be open to experimentation and adaptation as you navigate your journey of self-exploration. Embrace the process of discovery and allow yourself the flexibility to evolve and grow along the way.

In summary, self-exploration through introspection and self-reflection is a powerful tool for identifying underlying causes of ennui and areas for personal growth. By creating space for reflection, asking meaningful questions, examining core beliefs, identifying areas for growth, and setting intentions for action, individuals can embark on a journey of self-discovery and empowerment, ultimately finding greater meaning and fulfillment in their lives.

Pursuing Passion and Purpose: Providing practical strategies for rediscovering passion, setting meaningful goals, and cultivating a sense of purpose in life.

Rediscovering passion, setting meaningful goals, and cultivating a sense of purpose in life is essential for combating ennui and finding fulfillment. Here are some practical strategies to help individuals pursue their passion and purpose:

Reflect on Personal Values and Interests:

Take time to reflect on your core values, interests, and passions. What activities or causes ignite your enthusiasm and bring you joy?

Consider past experiences, hobbies, and moments of flow where you felt deeply engaged and fulfilled. What common themes or interests emerge from these experiences?

Identify Meaningful Goals and Aspirations:

Clarify your long-term aspirations and dreams. What do you envision for your life in terms of career, relationships, personal growth, and contribution to society?

Break down overarching goals into smaller, actionable steps. Set SMART goals (Specific, Measurable, Achievable, Relevant, Time-bound) to provide clarity and direction.

Explore New Opportunities and Experiences:

Step outside of your comfort zone and explore new interests and activities. Take classes, attend workshops, or join clubs and communities related to your passions.

Embrace curiosity and experimentation. Be open to trying new things and learning from both successes and failures along the way.

Find Purpose in Service and Contribution:

Explore opportunities for service and contribution to others. Volunteer for causes that resonate with your values and interests, or get involved in community initiatives.

Consider how your talents, skills, and passions can be used to make a positive impact in the world. Find meaning in helping others and contributing to something larger than yourself.

Create a Personal Mission Statement:

Craft a personal mission statement that encapsulates your values, passions, and aspirations. Define your purpose and vision for the future in a concise and inspiring statement.

Use your mission statement as a guiding compass to make decisions and prioritize activities that align with your core values and goals.

Practice Self-Compassion and Persistence:

Be patient and compassionate with yourself as you navigate your journey of rediscovering passion and purpose. Embrace setbacks and challenges as opportunities for growth and learning.

Cultivate resilience and persistence in the pursuit of your goals. Stay focused on your vision, and celebrate progress, no matter how small, along the way.

Seek Support and Accountability:

Surround yourself with a supportive network of friends, family, mentors, and peers who encourage and uplift you in your pursuit of passion and purpose.

Share your goals and aspirations with others and enlist their support in holding you accountable to your commitments and staying motivated.

Practice Gratitude and Celebration:

Cultivate a mindset of gratitude for the opportunities, resources, and experiences that support your journey. Take time to acknowledge and celebrate your achievements and milestones.

Regularly reflect on the progress you've made and the positive impact you've had on yourself and others. Find joy and fulfillment in the pursuit of your passion and purpose.

By implementing these practical strategies, individuals can rediscover their passion, set meaningful goals, and cultivate a sense of purpose in life, leading to greater fulfillment, happiness, and resilience in the face of ennui and existential restlessness.

Embracing Change: Emphasizing the importance of embracing change, taking risks, and stepping outside of comfort zones to break free from the cycle of ennui and stagnation.

Embracing change, taking risks, and stepping outside of comfort zones are essential steps in breaking free from the cycle of ennui and stagnation. Here's why it's important and practical strategies to do so:

Why Embrace Change:

Change is inevitable and often brings growth, learning, and new opportunities. Embracing change allows individuals to adapt to evolving circumstances, cultivate resilience, and discover new aspects of themselves.

Remaining stagnant and resistant to change can lead to feelings of ennui and dissatisfaction. By embracing change, individuals can break free from the monotony of routine and open themselves up to a world of possibilities and potential.

Strategies for Embracing Change:

Cultivate a Growth Mindset: Adopt a mindset that sees challenges as opportunities for growth and learning. Embrace the belief that you have the ability to adapt, learn, and thrive in the face of change.

Step Outside of Your Comfort Zone: Challenge yourself to try new experiences, take on unfamiliar tasks, and explore uncharted territories. Pushing past your comfort zone fosters personal growth, resilience, and self-discovery.

Practice Flexibility and Adaptability: Develop the ability to adapt to changing circumstances and embrace uncertainty. Cultivate flexibility in your thinking and behavior, allowing you to navigate change with grace and resilience.

Set Bold Goals: Set ambitious goals that inspire and motivate you to stretch beyond your current limitations. Break down larger goals into smaller, actionable steps, and celebrate progress along the way.

Embrace Failure as a Learning Opportunity: Embrace failure as a natural part of the growth process. View setbacks as valuable learning experiences that provide insight, feedback, and opportunities for course correction.

Seek New Perspectives: Surround yourself with diverse perspectives and viewpoints that challenge your assumptions and broaden your horizons. Engage in conversations with people from different backgrounds, cultures, and experiences.

Stay Open to Serendipity: Remain open to unexpected opportunities and serendipitous encounters that may lead to new pathways and possibilities. Cultivate a sense of curiosity and wonder, allowing yourself to be receptive to the magic of life's surprises.

Practice Self-Compassion: Be kind and compassionate with yourself as you navigate change and uncertainty. Treat yourself with the same empathy and understanding that you would offer to a close friend facing similar challenges.

By embracing change, taking risks, and stepping outside of comfort zones, individuals can break free from the cycle of ennui and stagnation, unlocking new opportunities for growth, fulfillment, and self-discovery. As you embark on this journey of embracing change, remember to be patient, resilient, and kind to yourself, knowing that every step forward is a step toward greater authenticity, vitality, and purpose in life.

CHAPTER SIX
The Evolution of Ennui

Ennui in the 21st Century: Reflecting on how ennui has evolved in the digital age and its implications for mental health and well-being.

Ennui, or existential boredom and dissatisfaction, has indeed evolved in the digital age, shaped by the rapid advancements in technology, changes in societal norms, and the constant barrage of information and stimuli. Reflecting on its evolution and implications for mental health and well-being sheds light on the unique challenges individuals face in the 21st century:

Digital Distraction and Shallow Engagement:

In the age of smartphones, social media, and constant connectivity, individuals are constantly bombarded with information and stimuli, leading to shortened attention spans and fragmented engagement with the world.

The constant stream of notifications, emails, and social media updates can contribute to feelings of ennui by fostering a superficial and fleeting sense of engagement with the world, leaving individuals craving deeper connections and meaningful experiences.

Comparison and FOMO:

Social media platforms amplify feelings of ennui by promoting comparison and FOMO (fear of missing out). Individuals often compare their lives to carefully curated representations on social media, leading to feelings of inadequacy, loneliness, and disconnection.

The pressure to present an idealized version of oneself online can exacerbate feelings of ennui as individuals struggle to reconcile their authentic selves with the polished images projected on social media.

Digital Overload and Mental Exhaustion:

The constant influx of information and stimuli from digital devices can overwhelm individuals, leading to mental fatigue, cognitive overload, and burnout. The relentless pace of digital life can leave individuals feeling drained, disengaged, and disconnected from their inner selves.

Excessive screen time and digital consumption can disrupt sleep patterns, impair cognitive function, and exacerbate stress and anxiety, further contributing to feelings of ennui and existential restlessness.

Loss of Meaningful Connection:

Despite the illusion of connectivity fostered by digital technology, many individuals experience a sense of loneliness and disconnection in the digital age. Virtual interactions often lack depth and authenticity, leaving individuals craving genuine human connection and intimacy.

The erosion of traditional community structures and face-to-face interactions in favor of digital communication can exacerbate feelings of ennui and existential emptiness, as individuals struggle to find meaning and fulfillment in a world characterized by virtual connections and superficial engagement.

Implications for Mental Health and Well-being:

Ennui in the digital age can have significant implications for mental health and well-being, contributing to feelings of depression, anxiety, and existential despair. The constant pressure to perform and present a curated image online can exacerbate feelings of inadequacy and self-doubt, leading to diminished self-esteem and confidence.

Digital technology can also serve as a coping mechanism for dealing with feelings of ennui, leading to addictive behaviors and compulsive use of digital devices as a means of escape from reality.

However, by fostering mindfulness, cultivating genuine connections, and setting boundaries around digital consumption, individuals can mitigate the negative effects of ennui in the digital age and reclaim a sense of purpose, connection, and well-being in their lives.

Future Perspectives: Speculating on the future of ennui in an increasingly interconnected and rapidly changing world, and proposing strategies for fostering resilience and fulfillment in the face of existential challenges.

Speculating on the future of ennui in an increasingly interconnected and rapidly changing world prompts consideration of how technological advancements, societal shifts, and cultural changes may shape individuals' experiences of existential boredom and dissatisfaction. Here are some future perspectives and strategies for fostering resilience and fulfillment in the face of existential challenges:

Impact of Technological Advancements:

With ongoing advancements in technology, the pace of life is likely to accelerate further, exacerbating feelings of ennui and existential restlessness. The integration of artificial intelligence, virtual reality, and immersive technologies may offer new avenues for distraction and entertainment but could also deepen feelings of disconnection and alienation from reality.

Strategies: Emphasize the importance of mindfulness and presence in the digital age, encouraging individuals to cultivate awareness and intentionality in their interactions with technology. Promote digital well-being practices such as setting boundaries, practicing digital detoxes, and prioritizing offline experiences.

Shifts in Work and Leisure:

The nature of work and leisure is expected to undergo significant transformations, with automation, remote work, and the gig economy reshaping traditional employment structures. While these changes may offer greater flexibility and autonomy, they could also contribute to feelings of ennui and existential uncertainty as individuals navigate evolving career paths and identities.

Strategies: Encourage individuals to explore diverse interests and passions outside of work, fostering a sense of balance and purpose beyond professional achievements. Advocate for policies that support work-life balance, employee well-being, and lifelong learning to promote resilience and fulfillment in the face of career transitions.

Cultural Shifts and Values:

Cultural norms and values are likely to evolve in response to societal challenges such as climate change, globalization, and social inequality. As individuals grapple with existential questions about the future of humanity and the planet, feelings of ennui and existential despair may become more pronounced.

Strategies: Foster open dialogue and collective action around shared values such as sustainability, social justice, and human flourishing. Encourage individuals to find meaning and purpose through meaningful contributions to causes they care about, promoting a sense of agency and empowerment in the face of existential challenges.

Embracing Uncertainty and Change:

The future is inherently uncertain, and individuals must learn to navigate ambiguity, complexity, and rapid change with resilience and adaptability. Embracing uncertainty as an inherent part of the human experience can help individuals cultivate resilience and find meaning in the face of existential challenges.

Strategies: Foster a growth mindset that sees challenges as opportunities for learning and growth, encouraging individuals to embrace change, take calculated risks, and step outside of their comfort zones. Promote practices such as self-compassion, self-care, and community support to build resilience and foster well-being in the face of uncertainty.

In conclusion, while the future of ennui may be shaped by technological advancements, societal shifts, and cultural changes, individuals can cultivate resilience and fulfillment by embracing mindfulness, balancing work and leisure, aligning with meaningful values, and embracing uncertainty as an opportunity for growth and self-discovery. By fostering a sense of purpose, connection, and well-being, individuals can navigate existential challenges with resilience and grace, finding meaning and fulfillment in an ever-changing world.

Conclusion

Embracing The Journey Toward Fulfillment

Summarizing key insights and takeaways from the exploration of ennui.

Through the exploration of ennui, we've gained valuable insights into its multifaceted nature and its profound impact on individuals in various aspects of life. Here are key insights and takeaways:

Existential Emptiness: Ennui manifests as a profound sense of emptiness, boredom, and dissatisfaction, stemming from a lack of meaning and purpose in life. It can arise from societal pressures, technological advancements, and existential questions about the human condition.

Historical and Cultural Perspectives: Ennui has been explored throughout history in philosophy, literature, and art, reflecting universal themes of existential angst and disillusionment. Cultural norms, socioeconomic factors, and technological advancements shape its expression and prevalence across different societies and time periods.

Psychological Underpinnings: Ennui is rooted in psychological factors such as existential angst, lack of purpose, and disconnection. It can lead to feelings of loneliness, anxiety, and depression, highlighting the importance of addressing underlying psychological needs and fostering resilience.

Technological Impact: In the digital age, ennui has evolved with the constant stimulation and distraction of digital culture. Social media, digital overload, and shallow engagement contribute to feelings of disconnection and existential restlessness, emphasizing the need for mindful technology use.

Coping Mechanisms: Various coping strategies, such as mindfulness, creativity, and seeking meaningful connections, can help alleviate feelings of ennui and foster resilience. Embracing change, pursuing passions, and engaging in self-exploration are essential for rediscovering purpose and fulfillment in life.

Future Perspectives: As society continues to evolve in an interconnected and rapidly changing world, ennui may persist as individuals grapple with existential questions and navigate the complexities of modern life. Strategies for fostering resilience and fulfillment include embracing change, cultivating authentic connections, and finding meaning in service and contribution.

In conclusion, the exploration of ennui underscores the importance of addressing existential challenges and nurturing well-being in an increasingly complex and interconnected world. By understanding its underlying causes, embracing change, and fostering resilience, individuals can navigate feelings of ennui and rediscover a sense of purpose, connection, and fulfillment in their lives.

Encouraging readers to embrace the journey of self-discovery, pursue authentic connections, and cultivate a sense of purpose and fulfillment in their lives despite the existential challenges posed by ennui.

Dear readers,

In the face of existential challenges posed by ennui, I urge you to embark on a journey of self-discovery, pursue authentic connections, and cultivate a sense of purpose and fulfillment in your lives. While ennui may cast a shadow of emptiness and discontent, it also presents an opportunity for growth, transformation, and reconnection with what truly matters.

Embracing the journey of self-discovery is a courageous act of introspection and exploration. Take the time to reflect on your values, passions, and aspirations. What brings you joy, meaning, and fulfillment? What are the underlying beliefs and assumptions shaping your life choices? By delving deep into your inner landscape, you can uncover hidden treasures and unearth the seeds of possibility within.

Authentic connections are the lifeblood of human existence. Nurture genuine relationships built on trust, empathy, and mutual respect. Reach out to others with vulnerability and openness, sharing your hopes, fears, and dreams. Cultivate a supportive community of like-minded individuals who uplift and inspire you on your journey. Together, you can navigate the challenges of ennui and celebrate the joys of shared experience.

Cultivating a sense of purpose and fulfillment is a deeply personal endeavour. Find meaning in service to others, contributing your unique gifts and talents to the world. Pursue passions that ignite your soul and align with your values. Whether it's through creative expression, meaningful work, or acts of kindness, infuse your life with purpose and intentionality. Embrace the journey with courage, resilience, and an unwavering commitment to living authentically.

Despite the existential challenges posed by ennui, remember that you hold the power to shape your destiny and create a life of meaning and fulfillment. Embrace the journey of self-discovery, pursue authentic connections, and cultivate a sense of purpose that resonates with your heart's deepest longing. In doing so, you will illuminate the path forward and awaken to the boundless possibilities that await.

.....***.....